Published By:
Jasher Press & Co.
www.jasherpress.com
customerservice@jasherpress.com
1.888.220.2068

Copyright© 2014
Interior Text Design by Pamela S. Almore
Cover Design by Pamela S. Almore

ISBN: 978-0692356593

First Edition
Printed and bound in the United States of America

"DEDICATION"

I dedicate this book to my father, the late Pastor William Thomas Wall Jr. He was a genuine, honest, humble man of God who shared this same spirit to all whom met him. To my family and especially my son Drake for his patience and listening ears during the process of developing this book. A special thanks to the members of the Olive Branch Missionary Baptist Church and the members of the Deacon Ministry, you all have truly been a blessing to me and my family. I have truly enjoyed working with you all. To the Senior Pastors in my life I thank you for your care, love and concern: Bishop Kavin Campbell, Pastor Abraham Lockhart, Rev. R.L. Blount, Rev. J.D. Mills, Rev. Matthew Robinson, Bishop Walter Ellerbe, Pastor Frank Butler and Pastor Waldo Robinson. I am so grateful and forever humbled that God has allowed our paths to cross. May the Spirit of God rest upon us all…. Amen

TABLE OF CONTENTS

"INTRODUCTION"

Grace and peace to the co-laborers of the Gospel I have been pastoring for more than twenty years. I have had many ups and downs over those years. Though there are many aspects of serving the people of God that I love, there are also aspects that have brought me to my knees in total surrender. There have been things that happened that I prayed for and those that I did not. As Christian leaders, we have been given the key responsibility to remain continually attuned to what the Holy Spirit is saying to us. The eternal destiny of millions of people depends on us hearing this living word, obeying it and leading those under our care to do the same. We must have a clear insight into what the times demand of us as Pastors. If we are not clear our Ministries will suffer. They will not only suffer and fail to thrive, but they will not survive. The rewards of being a Pastor are many. There is no other position in the world that has a higher honor than to be called upon by God to Pastor. It is a calling of importance and a vocation of extreme contrasts. It can be wonderful and terrible. It can be fulfilling and draining. It can bring great joys and unspeakable pains. Despite the potential blessings of leading souls to Christ, the job of Pastor is one of the most difficult, agonizing tasks there is.

My goal within the pages of this book is to help Pastors and leaders deal with the dilemmas of broken Pastors. It is my desire to help encourage the experienced Pastor while helping nurture the rising Pastor. A Pastor must know the "spotlight" of the pulpit, but not allow it to lead him to "puff" himself up. It is my prayer that "Pastor to Pastor" will bless you and your congregation.

Yours in Him,
Pastor Tobias M. Wall

Chapter One

"Don't Ever Give Up"

I was raised in a wonderful Christian home with great values and morals. Every Sunday evening my father would gather us around the floor model T.V. at 8:00 pm. We would watch the T.V. Evangelist Jimmy Swaggart. Many times the T.V. would be turned off and we would just sit reading the Bible. We prayed and read our Sunday school lesson. But now instead of sitting with my family around the television, I am sitting in the Middle East, in the middle of a war. In the middle of things I did not ask for, could never have imagined and will never forget.

I was twenty years old, a young man and a soldier at war. I was assigned to serve in Desert Storm. I had enlisted in the United States Navy July 5, 1988. My position was a Hospital Corpsman. I had spent all of my time with the U.S. Marine Corps. I'd trained at Camp Pendleton with the 3rd battalion. I was in the United States Navy and I'd never been on a ship. There I was in a Foreign Country not on vacation, but in the midst of a war. I must admit for the first time in my life, I was scared to death. I was told that once I hit the beach, my life expectancy was about twenty seconds. I can't remember one night that I had a full nights rest. Every day I could hear the air raid and sirens. I am still haunted by the sound even now. It rings in my ears to this very day, seemingly louder and more intense each time. I can recall the day I was called to the operating room of a triage unit to assist with surgery. There was an eighteen year old man that had lost both legs, torn apart his left side and lost his arm. I felt closeness to him because he was from my home state of North Carolina.

He was recently married. I suddenly realized I was standing in some type of liquid. Unsure what it was I looked down, shocked, I was standing in a pool of this young soldier's blood. Like still photographs, my life flashed before my eyes. Why was all of this happening to me? How could I be in this awful place? Then it happened, everything that I had learned growing up in a Christian home, trained in a Baptist church began to come back to my mind. Thoughts of me not making it out of the war and never seeing my family again quickly vanished. That was one of the many events that I encountered. All of them resulted in a lesson.

God has a purpose in everything that you go through. God uses the things that we go through as teaching tools. Every lesson is filled with faith nuggets. It was Paul that stated in Philippians 1:6, "Being confident of this, that he who began a good work in you will carry it on to completion until the day of Jesus Christ." Before I go any further I need to tell you that every promise comes with a price. There is no victory without a fight. There is no testimony without a test. There is no crown without a cross. There is no resurrection without a crucifixion. There are just things you have to go through to get your promise. My years in the Military were part of a process. Those days in the desert taught me how to lean and totally depend upon Jesus. My faith in the Maker, the Creator of all humanity was increased through that process. I had faithfully served my country. My years of service were complete. The next chapter of my life would begin just five short years later.

In June of 1993, I accepted my call to the Gospel Ministry. Less than a year later I was blessed to pastor my first church, Morning Star Baptist Church Charlotte, North Carolina. I was the youngest Pastor in the city at that time. Shortly after my installation, I was married. I was a new Pastor, a new husband and now a new dad. My first son, Tobias Wall II, was on his way. Another process of growth began in my life. I saw a wonderful relationship between my parents as a child growing up. It was my impression that if I followed their blueprint for marriage, I would have the same success. This was not so. We were both very young and lacked maturity. We were not meeting each other's needs and it devastated me.

One day I was the rising star of the east; the brightest star shinning, but just two and a half years into pasturing and marriage, I was suffering through a divorce. I was a Pastor. I was preaching and teaching the word of God but going through a divorce. How could this be happening to me? My father was a Pastor. My mother was the head of the Missionary Department. They gave me every foundation to succeed, yet I was facing a storm that almost caused me to lose my mind. In what seemed like the blink of an eye, I went from living in a house that was built for our young family to living in a cold lonely room at the Continental Inn Hotel in a not so pleasant part of the city. I had nothing. I slept in my car. I only had one suit, so I would arrive at church early to get dressed. I used to put on my robe so the congregation would not notice I wore the same shoes and suit every Sunday. In all reality I was homeless and I felt a sense of helplessness. I'd been preaching and pouring my heart out, yet I felt like God was ignoring me. I felt like He who had called me to do His will turned His back on me. I truly understood what David felt like in Psalms.

Psalms 22:1 David asks "My God, my God why hast thou forsaken me? Why are thou so far from the words of my groaning?" In this particular Psalms David is crying out to God, not only because he feels alone, but it is a cry to God who got him in this mess and now David feels as though God has gone "A.W.O.L." (Absent without leave- a military term that means you left without permission) on his situation. He felt that God had fallen asleep on his issues. David was going through one of the most tragic times of his life. This Psalms is a cry for deliverance from something he never would have been in if he weren't following God. Isn't it amazing that sometimes it appears when you are following God it you are in more of a mess than you were, before you decided to follow God's will, God's purpose or God's plan? Isn't it amazing that sometimes you follow God and then wonder why in the world you followed God? Where you end up is not what you thought you were going towards. In Psalms 22 when David asks "Why hast thou forsaken me?" he is not talking about the absence or the presence of God. When he says God you've forsaken me, David is talking about the activity of God. The Spirit of the text suggests that David is confessing to God that he feels God is ignoring him.

The reason that David felt like God was ignoring him was because he didn't see anything happen on the exterior on his behalf. This is the war between the flesh and the spirit. The war between what the Spirits knows and what the flesh has to see and feel. David acknowledges that if God is not responding to his prayer request then God is ignoring him. So David suggested that if God is not doing anything, then God is up to nothing. When you talk about the flesh versus the Spirit, the Spirit goes on the basis of what you know. The flesh goes on the basis of what you feel.

I must be transparent, there were times in Ministry when I really felt like walking away. Calls I used to receive from my co-labors stopped. Invitations to preach the word of God suddenly stopped and were cancelled. I was told things like they didn't check their calendar. I felt like I had been exiled to the Isles of Patmos. Friends that I grew up with no longer cared. Family members began to reject me. The church folk even held private meetings plotting their schemes to put me out. Deacons, trusted confidantes of the Ministry suggested maybe I needed to sit down and wait for the storm to blow over. I couldn't sit. I had a call on my life to preach the gospel and preach I did. I began to preach like heaven and earth was coming together. I've learned valuable lessons through storms. I've learned to follow the example of the eagle; rise above what I was going through. The Bible says in the Book of Ecclesiastes 3, "For everything there is a season and a time for every purpose under heaven."

I challenge you to remember no matter what you may go through, rise above it. Soar like the eagle. God would never allow you to come this far to lose. The choice is yours; you can peck with the chickens or soar with the eagles. For me, I choose to soar. Here I am eighteen years later, God has blessed me and allowed me to Pastor the greatest Ministry on this side of Heaven. I have been assigned by God the awesome task of Senior Pastor at Olive Branch Missionary Baptist Church, Marshville, North Carolina.

If I had to change one storm I wouldn't. It was in the midst of my storms I learned some of the greatest lessons of my life. If you are faithful to God, He will be faithful to you. As you face your next trial, keep your eyes on the only One who will carry you through. He's already at work right now guiding, leading, directing and providing for you every step of the way. When the next storm hits, you have everything you will need to not only survive the storm, but come out victorious.

CHAPTER TWO

"YOU'RE NOT ALONE"

IF THE ENEMY KNEW WHAT I WOULD BE AFTER THE STORM HE WOULD HAVE LEFT ME ALONE.

Those in the Pastoral profession are ranked among the top three in the world for suicides. The number of Pastors whom decide to end their life with suicide is staggering. They are young, old, black and white. Their age, race and gender do not matter. The rate at which Pastors commit suicide is depressing. The ones that lead and pray for us, our leaders and under shepherds are taking their own lives. Daily these men and women go to God on our behalf. They study for years to become better equipped to help us, yet we often turn a compassionate heart away from them. They live their lives under a microscope of criticism and sacrifice more than we will ever know. Yet in still each week they are physically, emotionally and at times, spiritually depleted. Somehow, they find strength to feed us the word of God and encourage us that Jesus will make a way somehow.

You're Not Alone

As Christians many of us should be embarrassed about how we treat our spiritual leaders. Pastors, church staff and their families endure great judgment at the hands of those they serve. Pastors live such fragile lives it's hard for them to feel like they can be close to anyone. This is a terrible tragedy. Pastors need friends too. We need friends who do not have hidden agendas; friends who do not use us in spite of our issues, faults and failures; friends who do not judge us based on our past; friends who will be there to talk about issues and struggles; friends that will lift us up and not take us down; friends that will pray for and not prey on us. The saddest part about this is when we begin to think we have found a true friend, we develop trust, believe in their intent to befriend us, consider them an important part of our lives and in the blink of an eye they begin to hurt us. We allow ourselves to be vulnerable and are inevitably hurt.

Situations like this and many others are the leading reasons Pastors suffer from a number of illnesses. The rate at which Pastors are diagnosed with diseases like obesity, hypertension and depression is overwhelming. In the last decade an increasing number of Pastors have become addicted to alcohol, drugs and anti-depressants. These addictions have caused their life expectancy to fall.

In August 2010 the New York Times released a series of articles focused on Pastors entitled "Taking a Break from the Lords Work". The articles lead to the compiling of the following statistics of Pastor burn-out by the numbers:

13% of active Pastors are divorced 23% have been fired or pressured to resign at least once in their careers

25% don't know where to turn when they have a family or personal or conflict 25% of Pastor's wives see their husbands work schedule as a source of conflict 33% felt burnt out within the first five years within their Ministry 33% say that being in a Ministry is an outright hazard to their family40% of Pastors and 47% of spouses are suffering from burn out, frantic schedules and/or unrealistic expectations45% of Pastor's wives say the greatest danger to them and their family is physical, emotional, mental and spiritual burn out 45% of Pastors say that they have experienced depression or burn out to the extent that they needed to take a leave of absence from the Ministry50% feel unable to meet the needs of the job52% of Pastors say they and their spouses believe that being in Pastoral Ministry is hazardous to their families well-being and health 56% of Pastor's wives say that they have no close friends 51% would leave the Pastorate if they had somewhere else to go or some other vocation they could do 70% of Pastors don't have any close friends75% of Pastors report severe stress causing anguish, worry, bewilderment, anger, depression, fear and alienation 80% of Pastors say that they have insufficient time with their spouse 80% believe that Pastoral Ministry affects their families negativity 90% feel unqualified or poorly prepared for Ministry 90% work more than fifty hours per week 94% feel under pressure to have a perfect family 1,500 pastors leave their ministries each month due to burnout, conflict, or moral failure.

After looking at these statics my spirit needed encouragement. To find it I went directly to the Old

Testament. I raced back to find it with the great patriarch of the Old Testament, David.

David was the son of Jesse. He was a warrior, king, composer, conqueror, organizer and a unifier of men. He was a man after God's own heart. David contributed much to the kingdom. As a kind of King Priest he united twelve often fractured tribes of Israel, stitched together the religious faith of Israel with his governance, collected and disseminated the great prayer book of Israel, the book of "Psalms." David was so great, that one of the most well-known titles of Jesus includes the name of David. Jesus was also known as the "Son of David."

I race to David for encouragement because David like Pastors had so many trials that one under ordinary circumstances would deem him unfit for his calling. David's life was been filled with a family full of issues; a resentful son, a weak father, rape, adultery and first degree murder. In Psalms 22 David gives us insight of what one feels when he feels like he is all alone and has every reason to throw in the towel. Many of us are somewhat familiar with the words of this text. Many thought that the words of this text flowed from the lips of Jesus as an original statement from Calvary cross however, this is not the case. It is the assumption that Jesus was speaking the words in the Psalms 22 from on the cross that He had learned as a child in Judaic culture and tradition. This text is not a song of Christ; in fact it is a song of David. It comes during a time in David's life when he is feeling discouraged, abandoned, deserted, isolated, desolated, rejected and by himself. He felt that God had left him all alone. This

Psalms in particular is a cry to God for help. David feels as though God has eliminated him. He feels as though God has dumped him. To get a better understanding of the text you need to take it out of the Christological context and see Jesus in the light of the psalmist not the psalmist in the light of Jesus. In the New Testament whenever one quoted the Old Testament it was because of what the reader thought the author "meant" in the Old Testament. In order to really understand this Psalms you can't focus on what the reader interprets as God's action. You need to understand what David was going through in this psalm to make the statements.

In Psalms 22, David is crying out for help. It is a cry for deliverance out of something that he never would have been in if he weren't following God. Isn't it amazing that every now and then you feel like you are all by yourself? Isn't it amazing that sometimes it appears that when you are following God it appears that you are in more of a mess that you were before you decided to follow His will? You must understand, in the text when he asks the question "why have thou forsaken me?" he is not speaking of the absence or presence of God.

This is a given because he is talking to God, therefore we know he is not talking about God not being there. David is talking about the activity of God. When he says "Jehovah, You're forsaking me," it suggests that David is confessing he feels he is being ignored by God. It's not that God is not there, but he feels ignored and the reason that he feels he is being ignored. David doesn't see anything happening on his behalf. This is the war that often occurs between the flesh and the Spirit. The battle of what the Spirit knows and what the flesh has to see and feel. David acknowledges that if God is not responding to his prayer request then God is ignoring him. David suggests that if God is not doing anything, God is up to nothing. There are many translations of the Bible. I like the message translation of Psalms 22:1-2, "God, God, my God, why did you dump me miles from nowhere? Doubled up with pain I call to God all the day long. No answer. Nothing. I keep at it all night tossing and turning."

Have you ever prayed to God and nothing appeared to be changing? When you talk about the flesh versus the Spirit, the flesh moves on the basis of what is seen, heard and physically felt. The Spirit moves on the basis of what is known simply because God says it. So often times we think that we are being blessed by what God is doing for us. Therefore when God doesn't do for us what we think He should be doing, we make the assumption that He is ignoring us. It is human nature to think that God only blesses us or knows us when He is doing something for us.

This is how we link God's presence in our lives with the amount of tangible stuff that we have. Equating God with stuff this is incorrect. Prayer is not about getting what we want from God. Prayer is about getting what God wants from us. God is God and besides Him there is no other! Do not you fool yourself into thinking that God needs you. God doesn't need anything from us. Psalms 50:9-12, "I will take no bullock out of thy house, nor he goats out of thy folds. For every beast of the forest is mine, and the cattle upon a thousand hills. I know all the fowls of the mountains: and the wild beasts of the field are mine. If I were hungry I would not tell you, for the world and its fullness are mine."

This lets us know even if God got hungry, He wouldn't tell. There is nothing we can do for Him. The cattle on a thousand hills belong to Him. God is self-existent; He doesn't need our faith. He is holy. He doesn't need our moral support. He is sovereign! He doesn't need our permission because He owns all things. He doesn't need our money, company or knowledge. God is everywhere at the same time. He is all knowing and powerful! He doesn't need our advice. He doesn't need our hope.

There is something God wants from us. He desires a relationship; a connection with God. He desires our allegiance, affection and attention. He desires to spend time with us. He desires that we cast all of our cares upon Him. He desires that we share with Him all that we may face in our life. It doesn't matter if we feel embarrassed or depressed. Many times we shut those around us out. We even shut God out. How can we develop a relationship of intimacy and communication with God when we shut Him out?

David understood the necessity of open communication with God; the ability to be vulnerable and honest even when he felt that God may not here him.

In Psalms 22:1, David says "My God, my God," he uses the word Elohim. This word means to deliver, so David is saying God You are not living up to the nature of Your name. He is saying if You are a deliverer why am I still in this mess. This is what happened with Pastors. We question ourselves and God's appointment for our lives. Many will ask "God if You anointed and appointed me for this position, then why am I having such a difficult time trying to carry out Your will? Why am I struggling to make ends meet? Pastors often sit by and watch members of their Ministries purchase new homes, cars and have financial freedoms. Pastors are plagued with required court appearances that involve our children while members are favored with their children going off to college.

These differences that we Pastors witness between us and members lead to a state of depression. We really are trying to figure out what is God up to? To us there are times that it looks like God is not living in accordance to who He is. Feeling abandoned and forsaken by God can land you in a dangerous predicament. The flesh will begin to tell you that God can't meet your needs. The flesh will influence you to turn to things, people, and substances that will provide you with a feeling of satisfaction that the flesh is searching for. It will convince you that you have needs that must be filled and since God cannot or will not fill it, turn to something else.

It is hard to maintain your connection to God, when you feel so disconnected, but we must. In order to ensure we remain connected to God and avoid falling into the traps given to by the flesh, we must keep a cool head. The key to keeping a cool head when you are in a world of despair is to remember the character of God. You must not only remember it, but rehearse it often. You are a chosen man or woman of God. You are equipped by the great Author and

Finisher of our faith. God would never appoint you to a position that He would not give you the tools to be successful in. You must apply the same encouragement to your own life about God's comforting, providing and provisionary Spirit that is delivered to others through preaching and teaching of the gospel. God has not abandoned you. God is always with you. Every Pastor will have struggles. Often times they may seem larger and deeper than the ones before. Do not be fooled by this. It is a pivotal part of our journey as Christians and even more so as Pastors.

Satan wants to take every Pastor out. He wants anyone and everyone who has the ability to spread the gospel of Jesus stopped immediately and he will go through great lengths to see this mission through. Therefore you must remember you're not the only person with a giant target on your back. Every Pastor you have ever come in contact with have had or will have the same struggle with feeling abandoned by God. You do not have to carry this burden alone. Call a fellow Pastor, vent and share your struggles together. It is possible that your like struggles will bless each other and allow you to strengthen each other and inevitably bless the kingdom of God. Remember you are not in this alone.

CHAPTER THREE

"I DIDN'T CHOOSE THIS"

P astors have a very close relationship with God. We have a love for God and for people that is unconditional. We have the ability to serve, pray and encourage people through proclaiming the gospel. Many people say that being a Pastor is the dream job. We have front row seats to a lifetime of leading people to build their faith in Jesus Christ. It is a wonderful and fulfilling calling. Others only see the positives of being a Pastor. They see the ability to stand before a crowd and demand the attention of hundreds, even thousands of people; the chance to read the bible all day long, pray for people, drink juice during service and have people carry your bags as a great gift. While all of the listed items are blessings, being a Pastor is hard work.

Being a Pastor is a unique challenge. It's not for the weak and weary, nor is it for the faint at heart. People make foolish assumptions about Pastors. They assume that they can do the job of the Pastor better than the sent man or woman of God. I caution those who think it's easy to think about more than what they see when it comes to the life of a Pastor. The view of the pulpit is vastly different than the view from the pulpit. Prior to judging the ease of being a Pastor and how comfortable it looks to you from the pulpit, ask yourself these questions:

Pastors have the ability to be selfless and show a spirit of love to those that they know are trying to destroy them. Do you have enough love to look beyond their faults and see their need?

Do you have the will to get out of your bed in the middle of a good sound sleep to rush to the hospital for a sick member when the truth is you think it can wait until the morning?

Do you have the ability to eulogize someone that you haven't even met before or someone that tried their best to kill and destroy you?

The reality of a Pastor's call is it requires a heart that is after God, a life that mimics God's character and walks in line with God's word. It requires twenty-four hours dedication, seven days a week. Characteristic and lifestyle aside, the amount of time and dedication required is often too much for many to handle. This is why the position of Pastor is only filled by God when He calls, anoints and appoints the Pastor to his chosen Ministry.

The position of Pastor is not a job, it is not an occupation; it is a calling. The difference between a job and a calling are many. A job you can quit when you get tired, but a calling is who you are. A job you can call out sick when you are ill or frustrated. A calling requires you continuous and uninterrupted availability to people you know deeply and those you don't. When God has anointed and appointed you to serve, then you shall serve as God has directed. The calling of Pastor is 365 days a year, twenty-four hours a day. God doesn't care what you may have going on personally.

I will never forget a telephone call I received during a family vacation a few years back. It was summer. We had left for a week-long vacation. Two days into the vacation I received a telephone call that changed the remainder of the week. The telephone call gave me news that one of my members was just in a terrible accident. He was not expected to live. Because this was one of my members, I was immediately affected. I was heavy with concern for the family and with the idea that I needed to tell my children the news I'd received.

I had to break the news to them that our vacation needed to end. I had to face my children, who by this time had tears in their eyes. There they sat disappointed about the interrupted vacation and dreading the 5 hour drive we had to get back to the city. While juggling the fragile emotions of my disappointed children, I needed to focus on returning safely and calling out to God to strengthen this family for whatever they may face ahead. While my heart was aching for my children, it was filling with love, empathy and prayer for my church member and his family.

In order to lead God's people in a Godly fashion, the man or woman of God has to have a heart that is filled with love and compassion. King David gives us a prime example of how when one is called by God, it doesn't matter what you are in the midst of. You could be vacationing with the family, facing illness yourself, dealing with another's illness or like David you could simply be working.

King David was just minding his own business tending to his sheep when he was called out of the fields to be anointed and appointed to be King. King David was the greatest king that Israel ever had. There are 66 chapters that speak about David in the Old Testament. There are more references to David in the Bible than that of any other person. David's name is defined as "to be covered". David fits the description given in I Samuel 13:14,"But now your kingdom shall not endure. The LORD has sought out for Himself a man after His own heart, and the LORD has appointed him as ruler over His people, because you have not kept what the LORD commanded you." I believe with all of my heart that this mighty man of God has a heart after God.

The Lord didn't choose you, He chose him. As written in Samuel, God sought after Himself a man after His own heart. The point of your anointing is to please God's heart, not yourself or other people. You have to be anointed for the assignment. In the Old Testament, the term heart implies to emotions, reason and will. When God rose up David, he rose up an individual whose heart was directed by God's emotions, desires, and dislikes; God's reason of right and wrong; God's will to be done and not David's will. While in the Old Testament, the term heart implies emotions. In the New Testament, the word heart comes to mean a man's entire mental and moral activity. It includes both the rational and emotional elements. The heart is used figuratively for the hidden spring of a person's life. It is from the heart of an individual that everything should spring forth. Ephesians 6:6 says, "Not with eye service, as men pleasers; but as the servants of Christ, doing the will of God from the heart." Therefore those who do the will of God should never be those who are trying to win a popularity contest.

Those who do the will of God seek to please God whether they please others or not. It is not your mission to do things that will allow others to see you in a favorable light, yet those things that God will see as favorable. God is looking for people who are completely sold out to Him. David was so engulfed in God, that his life in public and in private reflected his love for the Lord. David sought after God's heart whether or not his actions were considered by others as good. When you study David's life you discover God has an uncanny way of taking a person who grew up not having the finest things in life, a person that learned how to struggle but still know how to bless the Lord all the time, a person that realized that he was where he was not based on merit, but based on the favor of God. God knew that when he called David from the fields that David's heart was chasing after God. When a Pastor is called by God, God already knows his heart. It is the Pastor that has to come to know the heart that God has known all along.

I love how Carlo Carretto talks about the call in his book called "Letters from the Desert"; God's call is mysterious. It comes in the darkness of faith; it is so fine, so subtle that it is only with the deepest silence within it that we can hear it. There is nothing more decisive and overpowering for a man or woman on this earth, nothing stronger than the call of God. This call is uninterrupted. God is always calling us. There are distinctive moments in this call and moments which leave a permanent mark on us; moments which we shall never forget. The call of God often brings about tension in the souls for many. The tension becomes a struggle with God that often includes more of us. The struggle can lead to old perceptions, unresolved conflicts and unanswered questions.

In our struggle with God, we also deal with personal conflicts, past failures, attachments to possessions, lifestyles, and our fear about the consequences of yielding to God. When we stop to think about humans contending with God, we're struck by what a foolish contest it is! One example that proves how foolish it is to struggle with God can be found in Job. Job must have felt the foolishness of the struggle when God inquired, "shall a fault finder contend with the almighty?" Anyone who argues with God must repent, Job 40:12.

Yet another story that comes to mind is Jacob's struggle with the Almighty. After years of successfully managing his uncle's herds and "mooching" along the way; Jacob decided to return to Canaan. After saying good-bye to his Uncles, he gathered up the family, his servants, his possessions, (and a little bit more than was his) and departed for his own country. As he came closer to his destination, his servants reported that his brother Esau was on the way to meet him. Jacob was terrified because he had stolen his brother's privileged place in the family. He prepared an offering to appease Esau's wrath. He needed only a quick memory scan to locate the fear he had felt when he had left home to escape his brother's wrath. This fear may have fed on his more recent cheating and greed during the breeding season. He had given special attention to his own cattle goats and sheep and neglected his uncle's interests.

Jacob had reason to be afraid. Before the fateful day of meeting, Jacob sent Esau gifts from his herds. His servants spaced the gifts just far enough apart that Esau received one peace offering after another. As another protective measure Jacob divided his remarrying estate into two camps. With this division if Esau attacked him and won he wouldn't lose everything. After making these preparations Jacob took his immediate family and crossed over the Jabbok River for the night. The story in Genesis continues, "Jacob was left alone, and a man wrestled with him until day break", Genesis 32:24.

If we had only this statement describing the struggle we might think that this man was one of Esau's soldiers or one of Jacob's own servants or perhaps represented Jacob struggling with internal conflict, but these speculations would miss the mark. Jacob was wrestling with a transcendent figure either an angel or the Almighty. He struggles with the heavenly visitor until the sun was coming up. Then the transcendent figure cried out, "let me go for the day is breaking" but Jacob responded, "I will not let you go unless you bless me." The transcendent figure asked "what is your name?" "Jacob" he responded. Then the figure decided you shall no longer be called Jacob, you shall be called Israel for you have striven with God and with human and have prevailed "and he blessed Jacob".

This brief narrative depicts a man who had been called by God to possess the land that had been given to his grandfather Abraham. He was compelled to respond to the call, but the call awakened his memories and unleashed his fears. He felt not only fearful of his brothers but guilty before God. He felt inadequate for the task and fearful of the outcome. This struggle drove him to prayer which is symbolized in his night of wrestling with the figure who eventually blessed him. Just how many times has this dramatic struggle been played out in the lives of God's people? Jacob prevailed not by overturning God's plan but by getting himself aligned with it. The blessings were indeed the Shalom or peace of God. In numerous ways Jacob's experience is paradigmatic to our own struggles with the call of God. Jacob's life had been changed overnight by yielding to the will of God's call.

Now here you are in the midst of night and with the twinkling of your eye, your entire being has changed. All that you knew as normal, your friends, your life and actions has changed. The call which you now possess you didn't seek; it found you and accepted you just as you were. No you didn't ask for it, but embrace it! Move toward being fully embraced by the call of God. We don't possess the call the call possesses us.

"DON'T JUDGE A BOOK BY ITS COVER"

The phrase or proverb "don't judge a book by its cover" was first used in an American journal in 1944. It was later used in a novel. Although it originated in the 20th century, a similar idea was used earlier in the 16th century. A proverb is a short, traditional saying that speaks of obvious truth. It is not mandatory that a proverb must always be true, nor is it universal to cover every possible situation. We utilize proverbs to express a brief analogy to explain a propensity. The proverb "don't judge a book by its cover" is a metaphorical phrase which means you shouldn't prejudge the worth or value of something or someone by its outward appearance alone.

One of the greatest lessons that I've learned in life and especially while on this Christian journey is that first impressions should not lead to lasting impressions. I've learned not to be too quick to judge based on outward appearance. I've learned not to be moved and manipulated or impressed by large churches, displays of shouting, dancing and speaking in tongues. I've learned that those who portray themselves as spiritual giants often end up as nothing more than spiritual midgets. People in Ministry often wear masks, but when valleys come and trouble arises it feels as though the enemy is not only at your door, but as though he has built an addition on to your home and has moved in. The mask you wear is fooling no one; it certainly is not fooling God or the enemy. It actually places you in a position where you are more susceptible to the enemy and his tricks. It places you in position where you must keep up the lies that are hidden behind the mask.

In 20 years of Pastoring I've had the opportunity to meet some of this nation's greatest preachers who have never pastored a lay church. This distinction does not equate to failure or success. The success is not measured by the size of the land, but by the God in the man. We often prejudge people based on the size of the things that they have acquired rather than the God they have acquired.

I too am guilty of judging a book by its cover. Over fifteen years ago I had the opportunity to meet a gentleman that I prejudged. I was working at a store that I owned called The Knotteshoppe. This was a boutique that featured designer clothing for men at a nominal price. The door opened and a gentleman entered looking to purchase suits and neckties. As the door closed a breeze filled with a musty smell drifted past my nose and along with the breeze entered a man filthy in appearance with stained clothes, dirty shoes and oil stained hands. Before he could get a good look at what was in the store, I started telling him about other suits that I had at home. I explained that he was welcome to come by and look at them. I would have told him anything to get him away from the store out of the path of other customers. A few days later as I was at home I saw a Lexus LS 430 pull into the drive way. I had no idea who it was and was sure no one I knew was driving this car. I went to the door to greet my surprise visitor. After searching his face, I realized it was the gentleman that was in the store a few days ago. This gentleman driving a luxury car was the same man I counted as a bum earlier in that week. I had judged him based on how he looked.

Turn for a moment to Zechariah. Zechariah was a contemporary of the prophet Haggai. He began his prophetic Ministry around 520 B.C. The name Zechariah was common in the Old Testament. The name Zechariah, meaning "the Lord remembers," was the eleventh of the twelve minor prophets. The book of Zechariah contains eight visions. Perhaps the most exciting and thought provoking is the vision that he experienced in chapter three. This vision virtually leaps from the pages. Zechariah 3:1," And he showed me Joshua the high priest standing before the angel of the LORD, and Satan standing at his right hand to resist him."

In this text Joshua is the high priest. This is not the son of Nun. This is not Joshua the assistant and successor of Moses. This is not Joshua the one that wrote the book of Joshua. This is Joshua that Zechariah had seen in the vision was son of Jehozadam. This Joshua that is tucked away in the history of the Old Testament was seen in this vision rightfully standing before the angel of the Lord. After all this, he was God's man. His life was dedicated to Ministry and serving God's people. He was dedicated to training and

35

teaching them in the ways of the Lord. Who else should be found standing before the angel of the Lord? Where else should he be found, but standing on the threshold of Heaven? He's on the verge of walking on the streets of gold. He's God's Pastor and Prophet, but the text goes on to say that the High priest is standing before the angel of the Lord and Satan is standing on his right hand side to accuse him.

The high priest was ready and prepared to enter into glory; ready to transition from labor to reward. Prior to his entry, Satan showed up and began to give some accusation against this man of God. It is the number one goal of the enemy to give accusation against you. It doesn't matter if it is true or false. Satan is busy telling God what God already knows about his people. When it comes to God, there are no secrets about you. He knows what you've done and gone through. Nothing is hidden from God. Joshua, this High Priest, finds himself the object of accusation from Satan. Let's be clear, the accusations were not false.

Satan typically known as the father of lies, this time is not lying. He is accusing Joshua, in hopes that he will keep him from entering into heaven. Satan began to call to remembrance all that Joshua did wrong in life. The Bible says that the High Priest was covered with the filth of sin. What Satan was saying is how this High priest dare stand before the angel of the Lord as filth filled as he was. Filth filled? This was God's man, His servant, Pastor, and leader, standing in filthy garments. What happened to the dress of the High priest? Remember his wardrobe consists of 4 parts: the breast piece, ephod, sash, and turban. Now here he is standing before the Lord in filthy garments and Satan is accurately accusing him. Satan was right. Joshua this High Priest was guilty as charged. He had fallen from grace. However God told Satan take away the filthy garments from him. And unto him he said, behold I have caused this iniquity to pass from thee and I will clothe thee.

This vision represents the current condition of the priesthood. It is also representative of the condition of humanity. It is part of Satan's plan to bring up your past and to threaten you with revealing the mistakes you've made. The enemy's job is to accuse you of what you have already been acquitted. God has already forgiven you, so don't allow the enemy to hold you hostage of your past.

I feel a similarity with Joshua. In today's society Pastors face this same level of judgment. No matter how good we look on the outside, our righteousness is as filthy rags for I Peter 4:18 says "and if the righteous scarcely be saved, where shall the ungodly and the sinner appear?"

I send forth a wakeup call that no matter how holy you think you are or how holy you think you look, none of us are. How many times have people looked at you and saw how well you are dressed and said they wished that they had it all together like you? In your mind you were thinking if they only knew. How many times have you stood behind the holy desk just going through the motion? How many times have you pulled up to the church with the weight of the world seemingly bearing down on your shoulders, but to look at you it appears as though you have everything all together? I remember growing up our family had a living room suit. This suit was placed in our show room. No one ever sat in the room, nor did they sit on the furniture in the room. The suit was always covered with plastic. One day my mother decided to take the plastic off of the living room suit. When she removed the plastic, the fabric started to tear. We were confused why furniture that had never been sat on and had never been used would rip apart. My mother asked the gentleman at the local furniture store why this happened. He responded that the same plastic that we thought was making it look good, did not allow the fabric to breathe. When fabric does not breathe, it rots and will easily tear. When we covered the living room suit with plastic, we ultimately destroyed the fabric. It is like that with people also.

Many times we find ourselves covering up who we really are and not allowing our true self to be exposed because we are afraid of what people may say. We try to preserve the beauty of our outside or our "cover", but we destroy our inside or the "book" because of what others think and say. The great thing about the vision noted in Zechariah is although he had gone through a lot and was in a perplexing predicament, he was on the verge of ecclesial euthanasia. He looked like a mess, but in God's eyes it didn't mean he was a mess. This rings true for Pastors too!

CHAPTER FOUR

"THE SERVANT LEADER"

The servant of the Lord is the theme that develops throughout the prophecies of Isaiah, God's chosen. He is his faithful one, loyal to Him in a world of unfaithfulness. He is God's disciple under God's own tutelage called to carry out God's purpose on the earth. In the service of God, the servant suffers reproach, but patiently bears up, looking to God for vindication. Isaiah 42:1-7 says, "Behold my servant, whom I uphold; mine elect, in whom my soul delighteth; I have put my spirit upon him: he shall bring forth judgment to the Gentiles He shall not cry, nor lift up, nor cause his voice to be heard in the street A bruised reed shall he not break, and the smoking flax shall he not quench: he shall bring forth judgment unto truth He shall not fail nor be discouraged, till he have set judgment in the earth: and the isles shall wait for his law. Thus saith God the LORD, he that created the heavens, and stretched them out; he that spread forth the earth, and that which cometh out of it; he that gives breath unto the people upon it, and spirit to them that walk therein: I the LORD have called thee in righteousness, and will hold thine hand, and will keep thee, and give thee for a covenant of the people, for a light of the Gentiles; To open the blind eyes, to bring out the prisoners from the prison, and them that sit in darkness out of the prison house."

What is a servant leader? A servant leader is a servant first. It begins with the natural feelings that one wants to serve and then a conscious choice brings one to aspire to lead. This is sharply different from one who is a leader first; perhaps because of the need to acquire power or material possessions. The leader first and the servant first are two extreme types. Between them there are shadings and blends that are part of the infinite variety of human. A servant leader concentrates primarily on the growth and wellbeing of people and the communities to which they belong.

The servant leader shares power, puts the need of others first, helps people develop and performs as highly as possible. When we think of great leaders, we imagine victory. We think of excellence and success. We think of players that are carried off the court after the game winning shot. We think of the army captains standing at the top of the hill with his sword raised high or the preacher standing in the pulpit with a packed church building and an offering plate that is overflowing. These are all wonderful pictures of success, but are they true indications of what God sees as successful? When we think of success, we don't imagine washing feet as God did for his followers.

When the time arrived for Jesus to be crucified, he began to prepare the disciples to lead what would eventually become the church. He taught them one of the basic principles of leadership. John 13:3-6, "Jesus knew that the father had put him in complete charge of everything that he came from God and was on his way back to God. So he got up from the supper table, set aside him robes and put on an apron, The he poured the water into a basin and began to was the feet of his disciples, drying them with his apron." The entire church, which now covers a globe, would get its start from these men. They would be the means through which this message would spread. Everything hinged on their success. Jesus prepared them through the following principle of servant leadership:

Power – Jesus' servitude was given context of His power when God opened His mouth. When He spoke stars came out and light came into existence. This same God did not lay aside His power, instead He fully embraced it. We can only truly lay down that which we possess. Serving others in a context of power promotes trust and relationship.

Self-awareness - Many of us view serving or being served as an indicator of our status in life. You know you have arrived when somebody carries your bags, brings you juice, or cleans up your mess. When Jesus washed feet He did it so knowing exactly who He was. He came from God and He was on His way back. In confidence of His identity, He was fully able to serve in humility. If you are unwilling to serve those you lead, it may indicate a lack of confidence of who you really are.

Humility - The act of serving requires us to have a humble view of ourselves. Later the passage tells us that a servant is not greater than his master. Is there really any difference between you and the ones in which you lead? We are all human. We all have hopes, dreams, trials, tribulations, faults and failures. As a leader, you have been given the responsibility to lead others down the correct path. "Leadership doesn't make you better," it just makes you more responsible.

Getting Dirty - The first things Jesus did was to set aside his robe. In an age where man wore sandals and walked in the sand feet got dirty. I'm not talking about a little dirt between their toes I'm talking about filthy dirty feet. Jesus was willing to wash despite the filth associated with it. When we lead by serving, we have to be willing to get in the mess and get dirty. Being a servant can be a messy job, but it has to be done. If we are never willing to get messy, we will never build trust in God's people. If we never build trust, our influence will be limited.

A Servant's Love - It is possible to serve with the wrong motivation. Jesus was not trying to manipulate these men to advance his own case and fame. His primary motivation was love. He served these men because of how he felt about them. Eventually they did spread his name, but how could they not after experiencing such a great love. Servant leadership focuses on the needs of others and not of self. Do you love the people you serve?

True Influence - The proof is always in the pudding. Consider what becomes of these men, of the twelve, seven were eventually executed. They made the ultimate sacrifice so that you and I could experience the realities of the gospel. Jesus had such a strong influence on these men. They were willing to die for him. This one act of leadership demonstrates to us true leadership. Soon after this Jesus did more than just wash feet. He allowed himself to be crucified in service to the entire world for that sin could be forgiven and we could be brought back into relationship with God. Dr. Martin Luther King said it best, "everybody can be great; because anybody can serve". You don't have to have a college degree to serve. You don't have to have the ability to make your subject and verbs agree to serve.

YOU ONLY NEED A HEART FULL OF GRACE. A
SOUL GENERATED BY LOVE.

CHAPTER SIX

"WHEN YOUR WINE RUNS OUT"

I have discovered that when it comes to managing our time, many of us are not good stewards at this task. In fact many in the Ministry find ourselves burning the candle at both ends. We find ourselves not using our time wisely. We tend to become easily burned out. Too often we find Pastors experiencing burnout. Burnout is a vicious enemy of Pastoral Ministry. It has the potential to damage relationships, leave people hurting, destroy marriages and even lead to resignations. Job burnout is not something that should be trivialized. The burnout syndrome attacks Pastors when and where they least expect it. It attacks Pastors in their relationships. It causes Pastors to withdraw from the very people they love. Part of my goal in this chapter will be to help Pastors and Ministry leaders learn how to deal with, relieve and avoid future burnout.

Take heed to yourself in accordance with Paul's exhortation to Pastor Timothy. In I Timothy 4:16 Paul was first concerned with Timothy the person before he was concerned for Timothy the Pastor. Many Pastors are reluctant to take an honest look at their own lives. Most would rather focus on the second part of Paul's exhortation; take heed to the doctrine and ignore Paul's command to "take heed to yourself." Translations pay careful attention to your life. Paul understood the wounds, discouragement and fears that besieged Timothy and afflict many Pastors. Pastors need to take heed to Paul's wise command to pay careful attention to you. Often we spend time visiting the sick, attending functions and paying attention to others while we neglect our own life. Take an honest assessment of your strengths and weakness. Be wise in providing care for yourself and your family.

Cultivate dependence in God to strengthen and empower the Ministry. Remember the Ministry is not yours, it is God's. He has called you and he must accomplish his work in you. Stop trying to control what you can't control and manage what you have no business managing. This includes managing others opinions of you and their reactions to you.

Lower your expectations and those of your congregation. Learn to say "no" and to delegate by asking others to employ their gifts. Biblically speaking, being a pastor is not a one man show. Have you turned it into one? Learn to balance your life and pace yourself. Remember that Ministry is not a sprint, it is a marathon. Take the long route and realize that sometimes slowing down will make you more effective. Create margins of time so that you are not always rushed. Take frequent breaks. Give yourself permission to take a nap and rest. Balance your time with your family. Although we feel that the Ministry can't survive without you trust me, it can. My father once told me after years of pastoring himself. "What would it profit a man to gain the hold world and lose your family?"

Regularly create time away to get refreshed. Why? Because your "job" requires you to be spiritually fit and you can't be in good spiritual condition by always being in the go. Jesus often "withdrew" to get a quiet place and effectively said "no" to Ministry opportunities; you should do no less. A practical way to actually implement this suggestion is to regularly schedule times of refreshment on your calendar and treat them as "real" appointments. If you are asked for a meeting at that time your honest response will be, I have an "appointment". Protecting these "appointments" is not being selfish, it is exercising good stewardship. It will increase your effectiveness and will protect you from burnout.

Cultivate interests that are not directly related to your work as a pastor. It is refreshing to engage in activities where you are not the one in charge, the one in the know and the one who must make it happen. Take up a hobby or a recreational activity; sports, gardening, fishing, carpentry, reading, biking, camping, hang gliding etc. These activities offer a healthy distraction from Ministry that will refresh you. It also provides an added bonus of the opportunity to develop metaphors and illustrations that will later be used during sermon prep and counseling.

Develop a sense of humor so that you can laugh at difficult situations. Laughter is an antidote to cynicism and sarcasm. Pay careful attention to your diet, exercise, and sleep patterns. Don't underestimate the importance of staying physically fit and daily exercise. Endorphins are God's natural high. Achieve endorphin release through vigorous exercise and exertion of energy.

Seek intimate fellowship with pastors and others with whom you can share your burdens. A common theme I see in counseling Pastors is their sense of isolation and loneliness. This only exacerbates their problems. There are likely many other Pastors in your city and town that face the same since of isolation. They are enduring similar struggles. Seek them out and cultivate deep relationships with them. Share your successes, challenges, and struggles. Don't buy into the lie that you "have to keep up appearances" and "protect your turf." Use wisdom in what and with whom you share. Protecting ones reputation is often used as an excuse to stay entrenched in isolation. By developing peer relationships you give God an opportunity to create friendships, alliances and Ministry opportunities on your behalf.

Get help if you need it. I know that you are used to being the one in control, doing the counseling, being there for those who are hurting and keeping everyone else together. I also know that some Pastors don't believe in being too "introspective". They see counseling as something that that "other people" need. You spend much of your time in the trenches with people who are suffering, helping them to overcome temptation and to deal with their personal issues and problems. It is those who are in the helping profession who are at risk for burnout. Recognize that you're getting burned out. In his provocative article, "Death by Ministry," Pastor Mark Driscoll stated that "it may be wise and appropriate to meet with a Biblical counselor to get insight on your own life and tendencies."

One of the best things you can do for your Ministry, yourself and your family, may be to visit with a trusted counselor who can be there for you, provide insight and feedback and help you along the way. My brothers and my sisters, we spend so much time doing things that really don't matter, when it comes to the kingdom, we can't handle the things that really do mater. There are times I find myself doing things that are not edifying the kingdom of God. Every now and then I lose my zeal. My will to go on and my determination are shaken. It almost feels like I'm running out of wine.

In John gospel chapter 2, the text paints for us a metaphor of the world we live in. It parallels the current situation that many of us find ourselves in each and every day. The text describes a marriage feast taking place. At such feats it was customary to serve wine as the drink. Shortly after the feast began a tragic thing happens. After only three days into the week-long celebration the wine runs out. That's what happens in many of our lives today. Soon after you start serving the Lord, doing his will, turning from sin, proclaiming the gospel and abandoning all for the call of Jesus Christ, your wine begins to run out. The feast represents the celebration of new life in Christ Jesus. Remember wine was the customary drink at wedding feasts. Just as a man and woman are joined in marriage so are we in Christ at the time of our salvation. What I'm trying to say is that your new life in Christ Jesus ought to be like a wedding feast or a celebration. It should be like a honeymoon that never ends. The honeymoon period in the pastorate is the time in which the Pastor and member is the apple of each other's eye. It is a period in which you are walking hand in hand basking in the love of each other. The wine that is being served is symbolic of your joy, peace, love and hope in Jesus Christ.

The wine is indicative of what everybody who has yielded to the call of the gospel will face. Too often we find ourselves running out of wine, running out of joy. We look good on the outside, but on the inside we are empty. We've run out of hope. We've become spiritually bankrupt; empty, depleted and exhausted and there is nothing left in storage, nothing left for us to pull from. As a result our preaching becomes passive. Our teaching is tired. Our witness is weak. Our worship is watered down. Our prayers are powerless. We're running out of wine. If you search the customs of feasts and celebrations, you'll find that running out of wine was an indictment for the family who hosted the feast. It was unthinkable for the host to run out of wine.

It is sad that so many of our leaders are running out of wine. It is an indictment on the church when leaders lose their love for Ministry. When you lose your peace, vision and passion for the kingdom of God it is tragic. When we start spending more time fighting the wolves rather than feeding the sheep you are running out of wine. How do you restore the joy of your salvation? You find the source.

Mary knew where to go. She knew what she had to do. She didn't waste time fooling with anyone else. She knew the source. I caution you about spending time with people who are not going anywhere. We were given the source upon our profession of our faith and such as it were with Mary. She went to Jesus. Now two thousand years later we still have access to the same source. We have authority to go directly to Jesus for He is indeed our source. Genesis 1:1 says "in the beginning God created the heaven and the earth." Jesus says in Revelation "I am the Alpha and Omega the beginning and the end says the Lord which is and which was. And which is to come, the almighty."

That's proof in itself that Jesus is still the source. When the world is turned upside down "preach". When hell is hovering right over your head "preach". When it seems like you are running out of wine go to the source, stay in the word of God. When reading the Bible becomes a job and not a love for God you will soon lose your love for Ministry. Now that you know that God is the source follow the recipe.

They had run out of wine, but Jesus said fill the water pot with water. The water pot represents a vessel (that's you and me) hard, empty vessels ready for use. Like wine the water is symbolic of the word of God. Jesus said fill the water pots with water. When your wine runs out you have to fill yourself with the word of God. When you fill yourself with the word of God you'll be able to say like David says in Psalms 1:1, "but his delight is in the law of the Lord and is his law he meditates day and night." When we fill ourselves with the word it becomes part of our inner person. It infiltrates us. When we fill up on the word it will become more than just words pinned to paper. It will become a living, breathing and life changing word. Now that you have found the source and you've followed the recipe, feast on the good wine for the Bible says that the headwaiter called the bridegroom and told them you've saved the best wine for last.

CHAPTER SEVEN

"HOLD UP UNDER PRESSURE"

66 "If you are going through hell keep going,"
Winston Churchill. We live in a time and age that
no matter who you are or what you do as a
profession; life will present its share of problems. This
Christian journey is not about giving up, throwing in the
towel or waving your flag in defeat. This pilgrim's journey
is not about running and hiding from the trials and
tribulations of this world. It is not about quitting; rather it is
about enduring until the end.

When I was growing up I noticed that my mother
often times cooked with a pressure cooker. I learned later in
life that a pressure cooker worked on a simple principle:
steam. A pressure cooker was a sealed pot with a lot of
steam inside. It built up high pressure which helps food
cook faster. That is how life is. When one is placed under
the pressures of life you mature and grow. The Apostle
Peter is a great example of holding up under pressure.

Luke allows us to look inside the prison cell of the Apostle Peter as he spends the night on death row. In one of my favorite passages in the bible Acts chapter 12, Peter has been placed in prison by Herod Agrippa. Herod is his title. Agrippa is his name. This is Herod the king: not Herod the great that show the infants at Bethlehem. He is not Herod Antipas, he who beheaded John. Herod Agrippa, the grandson of Herod the great and son of Aristobulus; this king stretched forth his hand to vex certain members of the church. Herod the Great and Herod Antipas had already made a name for themselves and now Herod Agrippa needed to do likewise. He needed to make a name for himself, but at the expense of James and Peter.

This is not James the half-brother of Jesus or the 59th book of the Bible; this is not James the author. This is James the brother of John, the son of Zebedee. Jesus tells us in Matt 20:22 that he should be baptized with the baptism he was baptized with. Meaning the baptism of Martyrdom; he was the first Martyr among the apostles. James has now been beheaded. Before we look at that account, take note of Luke's careful contrast of Peter and James. Both were leaders of the church.

When Herod began to persecute the church, both men became targets. James is taken in and immediately meets his end. It happened so fast the church didn't know how to react. Then Peter is taken. God clearly prevented Herod from succeeding in killing Peter. Passages like this go a long way to correcting any simplex notions we may harbor for how God may be predisposed to conduct our lives or answer our prayers for deliverance. There is no doubt there were prayers for James and no doubt James hoped for a miracle release, but none came. Peter didn't burden himself anymore worrying of rescue. The answer was simple; we will die sooner or later. Therefore the day of our death, having been appointed by God for His own purposes, cannot be a measure of God's pleasure. Not only do the good die young, they die old too (and the same is true for the bad).

God's decisions aren't necessarily based on our "goodness" or of displeasure. In this case, He determined that James' world was finished. But he didn't want to leave the church in Jerusalem without any leader in the city, so he spared Peter. James has now been beheaded. It was one thing to kill James, but Herod goes a little future to place Peter in prison and plan to kill him after the Passover. The king noticed that it pleased the Jews to vex the church. The king is not doing this because it's the right thing to do, but because it pleased someone else. There are those persons that do and say what they do because it pleases somebody else. This is an effort to gain temporary popularity with those whom are out to destroy you. One writer said it this way, this pleased the Jews, a blood thirsty generation of men, who had killed the prophets and the Lord Jesus and were now greedy after the death of the apostles.

Peter is in consolatory confinement. He's on death row. We all know Peter; he is the self-appointed spokesman of the twelve, water walking, fish catching, tent making, power preaching and knife toting Peter. For it is upon his confession that the church is first established. Because of his faith the disciples moved into another dimension. Peter who used to be the mouth piece of the twelve is now standing in the need of prayer. Water walking Peter is now walking the green mile. Peter is in prison and sixteen soldiers are assigned to watch him. The squad of guards assigned to Peter included two chained to him.

The reason for such strong guarding was because somebody had remembered that Peter and the rest of the apostles, who were committed to the same prison some time ago, were delivered. The Bible says in Acts 5:19, "but during the night an angel of the Lord opened the doors of the jail. And brought them out." Peter is due to die in the morning. He is the next man up for execution. Peter is not on his knees praying. He is not complaining. He is not trying to get the governor to stay his execution. The brother is sleeping. Isn't this strange? Peter has a habit of sleeping when he should be praying. Peter is due to die in the morning but the night before, he trusted in the Lord. While he slept the church prayed to the Holy Spirit to make intercession on his behalf.

Peter was in trouble so the church began to pray. As they were praying Peter was being set free. Because of a praying church Peter shows up on the door steps of Martha's house. But while they were praying in Mary and Martha's house, in the prison an angel appeared in the room and commanded Peter to walk out. The chain fell off his wrist and the angels commanded him to get dressed. This was such a miraculous movement that Peter thought he was dreaming. One moment he was in chains, the next he was free. He went to sleep in a bad situation and work up in a better situation. Peter that was on death row, now had the ability to knock at the door of the home where his people prayed him free. The maid name Rhoda went to the gate to answer when she saw Peter. She was excited at the sight of Peter. She left him to hurry and tell the others. The rest of the brethren are equally surprised and don't believe her at first. They said it must be an angel because Jewish belief at the time held that every person had a guardian angel and these angels resembled the person. They assumed she saw Peter's angel rather than Peter himself. The late Dr. C.A.W. Clark of the Good St. Baptist Church in Dallas, Texas advised that the angels left heaven in an unconceivable rapidity to release the apostle and the angels escorted him out of the prison. I often wondered which view requires more faith; the church who prayed to God to set Peter free or Peter who simply slept and trusted God. Whatever the case the results were the same Peter trusted God under pressure.

Money, cars, clothing and houses are good but like Peter, what the Pastor needs most is prayer. The church should pray for its Pastor like they prayed for Peter. When the church prays for its Pastors, it will dismantle the fiery darts of the enemy. When the church prays for its Pastors, their enemies will become their foot stool. When the church prays for its Pastors, they will be freed from the bondage of the enemy and walk freely within God's will. The reason the enemy is on your track and trying to destroy your destiny is because of what is on the inside of you. He sees greatness, he sees vision and he sees that you are the head. The reason that the devil is trying to knock you out of the fight is because he knows that you are a survivor. The enemy knows that if you survived it before you will survive it again. It does not matter what situation or circumstance, dilemma of difficulties, when you turn it over to Jesus, He will work it out. The Bible declares in Psalms, those who trust in the Lord are as secure as Mount Zion. They will not be defeated but will endure forever. If you trust in the Lord, you can sleep through anything. David said "I took my troubles to the Lord; I cried out to Him and He answered my prayer."

I'm unsure of your place in life, but what I am sure of is that God never fails us. God either does one of two things while we are going through life. He will either lift burdens or make our shoulders strong enough to carry them. I leave you with this quote, "To live your best life now, you must learn to trust God's timing. You may not be sure of this right now, but behind the scenes God is arranging all the pieces to come together to work out life's plans for your life." Author unknown

No matter how dark the nights, trust in God. Hold your head up. Even under the weight and pressures of the world stand firm and preach the gospel of Jesus Christ. Amen.

NUGGETS OF WISDOM TO GET YOU THROUGH.....

1. Our minds are somewhat like a transmission in a car. We can choose which way we want to go by engaging the gears. It doesn't take any more effort to go forward than it takes to go backwards. The decision is all up to you. You have to decide which way you won't to go. I'm moving forward in the things of God. Stop crying over spilled milk. Get the mop and clean up the mess and keep it moving. What's done is done.

2. You were not created to mimic somebody else. God doesn't want a bunch of clones or look-alikes. He likes varieties. You should not let people pressure you or make you feel badly because you are not like them. When you go around trying to be like somebody else, not only does it demean you, it steals your uniqueness. Be an original not a cheap copy. Dare to be different. Be what God has created you to be. You are so beautiful in the sight of God.

3. Live with and attitude of faith; before long God's favor is going to show up and that difficult situation will turn around to your benefit. Keep the faith and hold on, your best days are ahead.

4. Don't complain about what you allow. It's your choice. Choose GREATER for your life.

5. We all want to be free from our past and to do so you must understand this basic principle; the past is the past. You cannot do anything to undo what has happened in your past. You cannot relive one moment of your past. But you can do something about it right now. Your attitude should be I refuse to dwell on the negative things that have happened to me. I am not going to think about all that I have lost. I am going to focus on what could have been or should have been. Today is a good day and it is going to be the beginning of a great life.

6. The past has no power over the present. Don't allow the enemy to hold you hostage in your past. The enemy is right, you did fail, you do have some faults and yes you made mistakes, "But God!!!!!!" You are not the sum total of your past. The Bible says, but as it written, eyes have not seen, nor ears heard, neither have entered into the heart of man, the things which God has prepared for them that love Him. Your Future is so bright, if I were you, I would invest in some sunglasses. Your past is powerless but your future is powerful.

7. I've been so blessed to be encircled around great men and women of God. It is amazing what can happen when you get into an atmosphere where people build you up rather than tear you down; where people encourage and challenge you to be the best you can be you. It is so important that you spend time with people who inspire you to reach for new heights. If you associate with successful people before long their enthusiasm and motivation will become contagious. If you stay in an atmosphere of victory you will soon develop a winning mindset. You will soon become what you hang around, be it negative or positive. If you hang around people of faith your own faith will increase. It is your season, your time for you to soar with eagles rather than pecking around with chickens. Dream big, dream wide and God will take you places that you couldn't even imagine. And always remember you will win if you don't quit.

8. No matter what has come against you, or what is causing you to slip and fall, no matter who or what is trying to push you down, beat you down, drag you down or keep you down, you need to keep getting up on the inside. We are not created to live in despair, depression, defeat or denial. A negative spirit dries up your energy; it weakens your immune system. Many people are living with physical ailments and in emotional bondage because you are not standing up on the inside. My friends if you really want to give your enemy a nervous breakdown, I decree and declare if you stand up in Jesus' name you will have the VICTORY.

9. Church hurt is a bad hurt, but God's love is the greatest love of all. Stop putting your faith in man and put all of your faith in God.

10. Yesterday is history. Tomorrow is a mystery, but today is a gift, and that is why it's called the present. Live today to bring God glory.

11. The Lord said to tell you to take the limits off of Him. Don't restrict Him to past methods or past experiences or past manifestations. God is doing a new thing in this season and He's looking for people that will simply trust in Him with all of your heart.

12. God blesses us on a curve like that grade school teacher that gave a test and no one in the class scored above 70%.The teacher does not want to fail the whole class so she grades us on a curve. Every morning we wake up we are clothed and in our right mind so we think that because we are still breathing we have done it on our own but you've been graded on a curve. Nice house, nice car, fine clothes on your back, good health; you've been graded on a curve. The truth of the matter is God gave you a passing grade, when the truth is you really "flunked" the test. Thanks be unto God that He looked beyond our faults and saw our needs. Thank God for His mercy when we really failed the test, His love gave us a passing grade.

13. Talent is God-given, be humble. Fame is man-given, be grateful. Conceit is self-given, be careful. Use what He has given you to bring Him Glory.

14. I've discovered that God is more interested in changing me than He is changing my circumstances. Understand me, I'm not saying that God won't deliver us from our struggles by changing the circumstances. But most of the time, God uses trials and tribulations to bring us to the light of our impurities in our own character or areas in which we need to improve. God deliberately uses some situations as a mirror so we can recognize the problem in ourselves and learn to deal with them. The Bible says let every man examine his own self. The old song states you have to sweep around your own front door before you try to sweep around mine.

15. None of us enjoy going through storms and struggles, but you have to understand that your struggle may be an opportunity for advancement and promotion. The very thing you are fighting against so tenaciously maybe the springboard that catapults you to a new level of excellence. Your challenges may become your greatest asset. The greater the storm, the greater the blessing.

16. When negative things happen for us no matter how much we yell, scream, murmur and complain it will not make it better. We might as well keep our peace, remain calm, stay focused and happy.

17. Rather than letting go of the hurt and pain we have experienced, too many of us attempt to bury it deep down inside our hearts. We attempt to cram our unforgiveness, anger, malice and hatred and other destructive responses into our "leak-proof" heart.

18. There are people in your life that are there only to bother you. These people are in your life to keep you on your knees. These people are in your life because they are a part of the problem and not the solution. These same people that bother you, frustrate you, antagonize you, bring you heartache and pain, tears and sorrow, will be the same people that catapults you into your destiny. What they meant for evil, God is going to turn around and make it for your good.

19. When you surrender your life to God and commit yourself to serve Him, you are not in charge of where He sends you. God is somewhat like the military in this respect. He will put you where you are needed. Trust God in where He sends you and you will always make the right choices.

20. Bishops, Pastors, Evangelists, Prophets and Elders that are in leadership positions should be aware of spiritual highs because it can become intoxicating and addictive. If you are not careful it will cause you to lose focus on your purpose for the kingdom. The applause of people will be so gratifying that you lose the glory of God. Because at the end of the day we are all servants of Jesus Christ and we are sent to serve God's people. Be careful of the little god syndrome, because it will kill your gift every single time. You are anointed for Gods purpose and not your own. Don't sale your anointing for applause and pats on your back. Amen.